WHEN GRACE & MERCY MET ME
God Cares

By Erica McGraw

KINGDOM NEWS TODAY
Publication Services, LLC

When Grace & Mercy Met Me
God Cares

Copyright © 2019, Erica McGraw.
Contact the Author via e-mail at KingdomNews16@gmail.com.

All rights reserved. No part of this book may be reproduced, stored in a retrieved system, or transmitted in any form or any means, electronic, mechanical, photocopying, recording, scanning, or otherwise, without the prior written permission of the author.

Author: Erica McGraw
Editor: Anjeanette Alexander
Publication Services: Kingdom News Publication Services, LLC.

DISCLAIMER

All the material contained in this book is provided for educational and informational purposes only. No responsibility can be taken for any results or outcomes resulting from the use of this material.

While every attempt has been made to provide information that is both accurate and effective, the author does not assume any responsibility for the accuracy or use/misuse of this information.

Printed in the United States of America.
ISBN 978-0998026251

DEDICATION

I would like to dedicate this book to my church family at God Cares We Care House of Prayer in Little Rock, Arkansas where my pastors are Pastor Willie Brown and his lovely wife Co-Pastor Joyce Brown. The idea for this book came while sitting in service and thinking about doing a skit for Resurrection Sunday. As I sat there, the Lord began to give me different characters from the Bible and how He extended grace and mercy to each of them despite their situation.

Special thank you to the cast who brought these characters to life on Resurrection Sunday 2019.

Introduction – Connie Lovelace
Eve – Junitha West
Sarah – Erica McGraw
Ham – Brandon Jackson
Lot's Wife – Desiree Dozier
Gomer – Samantha Lovelace
A Mother's Love – Miranda Harris
Mary – Louvenia Alexander
Peter – Arzo Johnson
Jesus – Daniel Johnson

Also, I would like to dedicate this book to my mom. She supports me on every project. Mom, I thank you for being my biggest supporter. I love you!

FOREWARD

We are all a part of a divine exchange. The exchange rate is wealthier, more priceless, and better than worldly treasures. Isaiah tells us to exchange our ashes for beauty, our mourning for the oil of joy, and our heaviness for praise. The greatest exchange happened over 2,000 years ago at Calvary. We tend to measure our worth by how many times we have hit or missed the mark of life. Not so with God. He says in the Song of Solomon 4:7(AMP) that we are altogether lovely with no blemish or flaw in us. He doesn't view us through our mistakes, sins, or wrong turns. God views us in through His love, grace, and mercy. He sees us as creations that glorify Him. Do you believe that is true for yourself? No. Well, let these well-known characters share with you how their lives changed when Grace and Mercy Met them. Erica McGraw has written a wonderful book that will take you on a journey to reflect on where grace and mercy met you.

Angie Alexander
Editor

INTRODUCTION

We are saved by grace, God's grace. His grace is also linked to His great mercy. Grace and Mercy are often confused, but they both are a gift from God Himself to each one of us. Mercy is God not punishing us for our sins. He withholds the punishment that we actually deserve. While on the other hand, grace is Him blessing us despite the fact we do not deserve it. It is His compassion and the extension of His kindness toward us even though we are unworthy of it. Isn't this amazing? It's all because He loves us unconditionally.

We have an advantage that those in the Bible didn't have. Many that we read about in the Bible were trailblazers. We have their lives to use as a gauge to lead us and guide us. We have the opportunity to learn from their mishaps and mistakes as well as their victories and achievements. Do you often wonder, WHAT IF? What if Eve hadn't eaten the apple, what if the lineage of Noah was able to be sin free after the flood, what if? It is through these questions of 'What If?' that this project came alive. I can imagine the people being remorseful of their actions if they could see how it caused generations and generations to deviate from God's plan.

Today, we are going to hear from some very familiar people of the scriptures as well as some not so familiar people. Each character will reminisce of how God's grace and mercy operated in their lives. Everyone has a story and a testimony as to how GREAT our Father in Heaven was to them. They are going to share how God had extended His grace and mercy to them, but they either denied it or did not realize or understand what was happening at the time. Some may have to say, "If I only knew, then I would have done differently." While others will just praise to God for seeing through their situation as they realize His protection was right there all the time. Finally, others will speak of the lessons they learned because of their behavior and how God continued to extended His love to them despite their behavior.

As you read, listen to how they share their hearts about the way they now desire to honor the work of our God and His Son, Jesus Christ and the Precious Holy Spirit.

TABLE OF CONTENTS

Eve	1
Cain	5
Sarah	10
Ham	14
Lot's Wife	17
Joseph	23
David	31
Gomer	36
Jonah	39
A Mother's Love	46
Mary, Jesus' Mother	49
Martha	53
Peter	57
Paul	65
Jesus	69

Eve

HELLO EVERYONE, I AM EVE, you know, the wife of Adam. I was created from his rib, and I was the very first woman on the earth. When God created me, He placed me in a grand, beautiful garden, the Garden of Eden. Life was wonderful; everything I needed was supplied. I lived in Paradise. There was no rain, yet all the plants and foliage were a beautiful green. We didn't experience any storms or natural disasters. My husband and I lived a blissful life, we were happy, in love and enjoyed our personal relationship with God, our Father, and our Creator.

Then the day came, the day I sold out to an invader. It started out a beautiful, sunny day. I was walking on the trails and paths in the garden, just admiring God's amazing work. I was in awe that it only took Him six days to create all that He created. As I was walking, the serpent came walking next to me. He began to ask me several questions and I answered them all, but then he pointed out the tree, the tree that I knew was forbidden. He said, "Oh Eve, why is that fruit forbidden?" I said, "I don't know, I just know that we were instructed to not eat from it and if we eat from it, we shall die." "You shall die? Do you believe that? What do you believe God is hiding from you?" I didn't know what to say, but I responded and told the serpent, "I know that God has taken care of me and he told me that this was the tree of the knowledge of good and evil. Adam and I just know that we need to obey God." Then the serpent enticed me by telling me that God is hiding something from us and that I should eat from that tree to see what God is really hiding from us. I must admit that I was in a moment of weakness. I folded and succumbed to the pressure of the serpent.

My attention turned to the tree, and I realized that the fruit on that tree was the same as the fruit on the other trees. Curiosity got the best of me. I began to see that the fruit on that tree was good for food, it was a beautiful tree, and of course, I wanted to be wise. Was the serpent right? Was God really hiding something from me? I had to go find out for myself. I grabbed a piece of fruit and ate of it. I also took it back home and shared it with my husband, Adam. As soon as we ate of it, our eyes were opened and we realized we were naked. Immediately, we heard the Lord call to Adam saying, "Where are you?" Adam knew he couldn't hide from the Lord so he spoke out and said, "I heard your call, but I was afraid because I was naked, so I hid." God asked us, "Who told you that you were naked? Have you eaten of the tree I commanded you not to?"

It was at that moment that our lives changed. Before then Adam and I worked and operated in unity, but Adam began to blame me and he immediately told God, "The woman you gave me, she gave me fruit from the forbidden tree." Then I said, "But God, the serpent tricked me and I ate." God was not pleased. Adam had to go and work for the first time in his life. He had to tend the land. God cursed the serpent and made him crawl on his belly the rest of his life. As for me, I was told I would have great sorrow and pain bringing my children into this world and that my husband has rule over me. Life was not as abundant and free as it was. Sin had entered our lives, and we are reaping the consequences.

As I reflect back, I wish I would have had the strength to resist the temptation of the serpent because now I realized the greatness of God's will that was sacrificed through my disobedience. If only I had known the intent of the serpent to distract me and entice me, I would have done better. God blinded us for our protection because He loved us and nurtured our relationship with Him, but we let Him down. He gave us all those beautiful things in the garden because He loved us. The work that we were created to do caused Him to send His son Jesus to complete our assignment. We missed the mark, but if I had an opportunity to do it all over again, I would definitely do it differently. The sin seeds that were birthed in Adam and me were also birthed in the lives of our children. This sin grew and had been placed in all flesh born. It got so bad with our family that our son Cain killed his own brother Abel. If only I had known.... If only I had known, I truly would have done things differently.

I COMMITTED THE FIRST MURDER. I am not proud of this at all, but I took the life of my brother Abel. Please, let me back up and tell you my story. As you know my brother and I were the first two sons of Adam and Eve. Many who have studied our lives have come to say that we were twins and I was the eldest and Abel was my younger brother.

Our professions were quite different. Abel was a shepherd and took care of the flocks, while I took after my father and was a tiller of the ground. We knew we had to bring sacrifices to the Lord because it was something our parents taught us. See, after my parents sinned and it was revealed they were naked, God sacrificed an animal to cover their nakedness. In other words, their nakedness had to be covered and that was done from the skin of an animal. The bloodshed of that animal was a representation of Him sending His son Jesus to take away our sins in the future, but that was way past our time. But the scriptures did say that the wages of sin are death.

Our parents thought it was only right that since they had to give offerings for their sins, they too shall teach their children. We wanted to honor God, so it was even recommended that we not only offer sacrifices, but we give the best of the best and that our hearts be joyful while doing so.

The differences in our sacrifice is what caused me to be in disagreement with my brother and led to the worst thing I ever did. My brother gave sheep from his flock, and he brought the best sheep he had to offer to the Lord. I, on the other hand, brought fruit from the ground I worked, but it was literally from the ground. I gave God the spoils, the fruits that fell from the trees and vines that I had to pick up from the ground. They were already almost spoiled when they were gathered. Abel's offering was accepted by God, but mine was not. Anger and jealousy got the best of me because God respected Abel's sacrifice, but not mine. My offering was not accepted because I didn't give the best of the land. I gave God the scraps that had fallen on the ground.

The Lord even tried to explain what happened and why my sacrifice was rejected. He began by asking me a question, "Why are you so angry, and why is it that you look so annoyed? If you do well by believing me and doing what is acceptable and pleasing to me, you will be accepted; however, if you ignore My instructions, then sin will crouch at your door and you will become a slave to sin. Sin wants to overpower you, but you must overpower sin." Sin is like a sickness and while the Lord was dealing with me, I just couldn't focus on the lesson; to be honest, I heard what He was saying, but I just wasn't listening. I was just so angry at the fact my brother's sacrifice was favored and mine wasn't. This anger that was in me consumed me, and I began to not even think clearly.

I often wonder if in the anger that there was a fear within me, too. The fear that my brother, the younger brother was about to take over my position in the family. See, I was the older brother, which means, I was the leader. Was God's disapproval of me a way for my brother to win my rights within the family? Did God's approval justify Abel's rule over me? I just wasn't going to have it so; in some way, I felt justified to what I did to my brother.

So, this is what I did. I went to Abel and said to him, "Let's go into the field." It was here where I attacked my brother and killed him. Not too long after this happened, God said to me, "Cain, where is your brother Abel?" I responded by saying, "Am I my brother's keeper?"

When Grace & Mercy Met Me

Now as I look back, I see the error of my ways. Even after the Lord knew what I had done, He gave me a chance to confess, but I didn't see the grace He was giving me. I continued to lie. So He asked, "What have you done? The voice of your brother's blood is calling to me from the ground." I see how I allowed anger to live within me, and the Lord warned me about not allowing sin to rule over me. I did just what He was warning me against. That sin rose up in me causing me to do the unthinkable, murder. Now I had to reap the consequences of my sins. The Lord punished me for my actions. He said, "From now on you'll get nothing but curses from this ground and you'll be driven from this ground that has opened its arms to receive the blood of your murdered brother. You will farm this ground, but it will no longer give you its best. You will become homeless and wander the earth."

I cried out to the Lord saying, "Your punishment is too much. I can't handle this. You have taken my land and my livelihood from me and cast me out into the wilderness. Someone is going to see me and kill me. It's just too much." Now as I look at my plea to the Lord, I see how there was no remorse in what I had done to my brother. Abel was dead and I was focused on the punishment I received. I too deserved death, but the Lord spared me. He even promised me that if someone does kill me that they will pay for it seven times over. God had put a mark on me to protect me so that no one will kill me? Look at the grace and mercy He provided to me even in my sin, and I didn't even realize it at the time. I was so self-absorbed in my own emotions and thoughts that I didn't realize His grace and mercy.

I want to thank the Lord that even though He punished me and banished me from the land I was familiar with and caused me to leave my parents, He did not see fit that I should die for my actions against my brother. He extended grace and gave me hope. I guess that despite my actions, God did not see fit that I deserved death. Now I realize that my brother was just doing what he did because he loved and honored the Lord. His relationship with the Lord was a personal one while I was doing it out of ritual. I didn't take the time to understand what a relationship with the Lord afforded one. I may have missed the mark then, but I sure learned my lesson and I have made up my mind to reverence the Lord in all I do. Lord, I thank you for your grace and mercy.

Sarah

I LOVED MY HUSBAND, ABRAM, and believed in him. The Lord was always dealing with him, and he would come home and share these things with me. I remember one day he came home and told me that the Lord promised that I would become a great nation. This seemed a little strange because we did not have any children, and at our old age it was almost comical to think that we would have any children now.

Even though my husband had faith in God, when he was about 85 years old, he began making arrangements as to which servants would inherit his belongings and carry on the work once he had passed. He was close to his nephew Lot, so maybe he would be the one who would inherit his riches. But, again, the Lord began to deal with him and told him, "These men will not be your heirs, but a son who is your own flesh and blood." He continued speaking into my husband's life by saying, "Look up at the sky and count the stars. That's how many descendants you will have."

I began to realize the Lord was serious about what He was saying, so now was the time for me to interject with some assistance. I came up with a brilliant plan. I called to my husband and said to him, "The Lord has kept me from having children. Go, sleep with my maidservant; perhaps we can build a family through her." Abram went and slept with Hagar, and she conceived.

This brilliant plan I had now backfired. Now that Hagar was pregnant, she began to despise me. Of course, this was Abraham's fault and not mine, so I told him, "You are responsible for this wrong I am suffering. I put my servant in your arms, and now she is pregnant and despises me."

He didn't take the responsibility for what was done, he just said, "This is your servant and she is in your hands. Do with her what you think is best." This is when I began to be really mean to her, and she fled. Good, I can always get another maidservant, she is gone now. What was I even thinking?

The angel of the Lord went out to find Hagar and said to her, "Go back to Sarai and submit to her. You are now pregnant, and you will give birth to a son, and you shall call his name Ishmael." The angel continued by saying, "The Lord has heard your misery, and your son will be wild. His hand will be against everyone, and everyone will be against him. He will live in hostility toward all of his brothers."

Abram was 86 years old when Ishmael was born and finally had his son! A son of his own flesh. You see, something had to be done because no one was getting any younger. God kept saying he would have a son of his own flesh, and now he has just that. Sometimes a woman just has to step in and make things happen.

Thirteen years later, when Abram was 99 years old, the Lord appeared to him saying, "I am God Almighty, and I will make my covenant with you and will greatly increase your numbers. As for me, this is my covenant with you: You will be the father of many nations. No longer will you be called Abram; your name will be Abraham, for I have made you a father of many nations. I will make you very fruitful. I will make nations of you, and kings will come from you. I will establish my covenant as an everlasting covenant between me and you and your descendants for the generations to come. As for Sarai your wife, you are no longer to call her Sarai. Her name will be Sarah, and I will bless her and surely she will give you a son." When Abram was telling me what the Lord told him, I shouted, "What? We are old." Abram told me that when the Lord told this to him, he fell facedown and laughed and said, "Will a son be born of a man a hundred years old? Sarah's already 90. How is this possible?" He asked

God, "Can't Ishmael live under your blessing?" The Lord answered, "Yes, but your wife Sarah will also bear you a son, and you shall call him Isaac. I will establish my covenant with him as an everlasting covenant for his descendants.

There is so much more to our story, but I just want to declare that the Lord did exactly what He said He would do. He didn't need my help, and my help actually caused an "ishy" situation that all generations have been involved in. I want to thank the Lord for staying true to His promise given to me and my husband even when we were operating in disbelief. We were saying that we operated by faith, but our actions were far from it. We were doubting the power of God. He extended His grace and mercy to us and fulfilled every promise given to us.

Ham

My father was a great man of faith. He was laughed at and even called names like crazy and senile because he spoke of the rain that was to come and built the ark miles and miles away from the closest waterway. Hello, my name is Ham, one of the sons of Noah. God spared my family because of the honorable man that my father was. The world was evil and corrupt, but God saw something in my father that He trusted and my father was obedient. Many were living ungodly lifestyles; it was so bad that God Himself regretted that He had made man. God was so deeply grieved about the ways of evil having control in the earth that the most merciful act He could do was to start over and create a flood that would destroy every human being except our family.

When Grace & Mercy Met Me

My father was obedient to his assignment despite the heckling he received. After the ark was completed, God told my father, "I have found you righteous in this generation, so take you and your whole family into the ark." Wow, out of almost 750 million people, our family was the chosen family. Amazing!

Then God said, "Seven pairs of every kind of clean animal, a male and its mate, and one pair of every kind of unclean animal, a male and its mate, and also seven pairs of every kind of bird, male and female, to keep their various kinds alive throughout the earth. As soon as my family loaded up all the animals and all our belongings, we closed the doors and it began to rain. We were amazed because we had never seen rain before. The water filled the earth, and it rained for 40 days and 40 nights. There were times when we, too, feared for our lives. We didn't know what was going to happen, but finally one day the rain stopped. After about a week, my father sent out the birds to see if they had a place to land, but they would return to the ark. This let my father know that the waters were still high. This was done multiple days until one day the birds did not return. This gave us a sign of hope.

Time went on, and we were back on dry land. The earth was desolate, and our family was responsible for replenishing the earth. God had destroyed the evil of this world by causing the flood. Being part of this experience would make one think twice before doing something wrong. Let me tell you, sin is powerful. I remember one night when my father had gotten drunk and fell asleep naked. Instead of turning away when I discovered this, I ran and told my brothers. The sin that we were rescued from was rooted within me and has fueled the entire earth yet again. See, when I ran and told my brothers of my father, they went into his tent with a cover to cover his nakedness, they walked in backward so they wouldn't be able to even see him.

As I look back while sharing this story with you, I wish I would have exercised better judgment. I now realize that my family was saved by God's grace only to let the sin that was a seed deep inside of me hinder me from seeing the trueness of what God's plan was for me and my entire family. God's grace is so powerful, yet even experiencing it first hand, I missed the mark. If I had only known what God's will was, I would have done better. If I had only known the gift of life God had given to me during those 40 days and 40 nights and truly and sincerely thanked Him with a grateful heart, but I was blinded.

Lot's Wife

OH, DEAR HAM, please let me tell you my story. I lived in the midst of the evilness that was in the cities of Sodom and Gomorrah. People were warned of their wrongdoing, but that did not stop them. We continued in our sins. God was preparing His judgment for us, but even those upright and noble like your father didn't even understand that God's wrath was coming. The Word was going out, but it was falling on deaf ears. We sought pleasure over obedience. The earth was corrupt and filled with violence, yet we just continued in our evil ways.

My husband, Lot was the nephew of Abram who was very rich in cattle, silver, and gold. When Abram was instructed by the Lord to leave his homeland, our family followed. We dwelled together in camps with our flocks and herds, but discord started between our hired help, and we could not let that happen. Lot loved his uncle, but they could not agree on many things and they parted ways. Abram suggested that they go their separate ways. He said, "If you choose to go to the right, I will go left or if you choose the left, I will go right." Lot looked at his options, and he chose to take our family to the plain of Jordan. He chose to go in the direction of Sodom and Gomorrah, in order to obtain what he considered the best land. Everything in Jordan was well-watered and beautiful, yet wickedness filled the hearts and minds of the people who dwelled there. Lot did not consult the Lord for directions; he just leaned on his own understanding and desires.

As we arrived in our new land, we began to see and experience the evilness all around us. It was a prosperous area, but it was so wicked and grievous. Our souls were vexed daily with the filthy conversation and acts of immorality. People within the city gave themselves over to fornication and went after strange flesh of sexual immorality and perversion. People everywhere were committing adultery, walking in lies and did not even try to hide it. Shame was not even a factor, just the fact that we were happy and felt great pleasure in doing what we wanted. I believe now as I look back, God was warning us, but the evil that was present seduced us from clearly seeing the hand of God and preventing us from repenting. The grace and mercy God extended to our lost souls were not seen through our blinded eyes of deceit and pleasure. We wanted to do the right things, but the atmosphere of evil around us kept drawing us back into the environment.

One night while Lot was at the front gate, he saw two angels that came to the gate of Sodom. Lot knew they were not normal men. He recognized that they possessed great power, so when they got to the gate, he stood to greet them and then bowed down with his face to the ground. Then they came to our home. Lot held a position of authority within the city of Sodom and many from the city learned that these men were at our home. A large crowd of men, both young and old came yelling at Lot, "Where are the two men that came into the city tonight? What did you do with them? Are they in your house?" They got angry and loud and threatened to break down our door. Lot had gone outside to calm down the crowd, but eventually, the two men pulled Lot back in and struck the men with blindness. This is when the two men spoke to Lot saying, "Gather your entire family, sons, daughters, sons-in-law, and children and depart from the city at once, for it will be destroyed because of its wickedness."

Lot listened to this warning and did as he was instructed. He wanted to care for his family and do what was best for them. He didn't know that his desire to have the best land would cause him to have to uproot again to run from the evil that possessed this land. He may have had a little greed in his heart, but the time we spent in Sodom was not good for our family. The angels warned him to leave, and he packed up our family and we departed from the city. Our sons-in-law were not as believing or trusting, and they thought it was all a big joke because Lot appeared to have become a compromise. Lot acted in carnal ways, and his faith had become lukewarm. The actions of my husband did not act as one that was living separate from Sodom, but was an active part of the community. His backslidden lifestyle nullified any credibility he had with our sons-in-law.

Now, I realize that the heart of my husband was being drawn back to the ways of the Lord. I have learned to realize that when people speak of returning to the Lord and His ways, people will mock you. This is what happened between my husband and our sons-in-law. But morning came and the angels woke Lot saying, "Take your wife and two daughters that are here and leave immediately for the time has come for this city to be destroyed, and you don't want to be consumed in the iniquity of the city." At this point, Lot was struggling in his obedience. He knew the people in the city were wicked, but something there seemed to hold his attention. The sin of the city was speaking to the flesh of my husband, not only to him but to myself as well. Sin may offer pleasure, but it produces death. We knew in our hearts that we had to leave, but the grip of sin kept us longer than it should have.

The angels held on to our hands and assured us that the Lord is being merciful to us and allowing us to escape his wrath before he brings his judgment to the city. The angels said, "Escape for your life and do not look back." They gave us two direct commands: escape and do not look back. We departed the city and we began to run; it took all that was within me to not look back. The impulse to look back was just too great, all the memories, all the good times, everything I came to know in the city flashed before my eyes. My heart tugged at me to keep focused to keep these commands, but my will and the deep-seated root of sin craved one last look. It was a battle within that was just too strong to keep me from being obedient. We escaped safely before the destruction of Sodom and Gomorrah, but that battle within me cost me my life. I turned to take just one last look and immediately turned into a pillar of salt.

I don't know the exact reason why I turned back. Maybe I was just curious as to what was happening, or I was longing for the city and the lifestyle we lived. Was I testing God's command and didn't fully believe Him when He said don't look back? All I know is that God had made a way of escape for my family from the ways of the world, yet I couldn't comprehend it. He was sparing our lives and setting us free from the works of darkness, but my heart was blinded as well as my eyes. I wanted what I wanted, so in my selfishness, I lost my life. God had delivered us, we were on our way, but instead of now focusing on what was ahead for us, I looked back. I see now that I did not believe God's Word. I desired my old sinful ways and because of that, I lost everything. The decision that Lot and I made affected our daughters. We were not seeking holiness so that means we did not teach it to our daughters.

My heart hurts for the actions against God that I displayed. God's grace and mercy were right there for me to reach out and grab, but I chose to reject Him. If I had only known, I would live my life differently, I would not have looked back.

MY GIFT SAVED ME, not only me, but my family as well. That right there is enough to give God honor, glory and praise. The scriptures say that your gift will make room for you. Well, let me explain to you my story.

It's not always easy operating in a gift you don't understand. See, I was the second from youngest of twelve brothers and I was my father's most beloved. My brothers knew this, and they were very jealous of me. They didn't understand, nor did I. My father always said I was his beloved because I was born to him in his old age. He was about 91 years old when I was born.

When Grace & Mercy Met Me

I remember one night I had a dream. When I woke, I told my brothers, but they did not receive it well. I said, "In my dream, we're binding sheaves of grain in the field when suddenly my sheaf rose and stood upright, while your sheaves gathered and bowed down to it." This enraged my brothers, and one of them asked, "Do you intend to reign over us?"

I had another dream, and in this dream the sun and the moon and eleven starts were bowing down to me. I told my brothers and my father about this dream. My father rebuked me by asking, "What is this dream you had? Will your mother and I and your brothers actually come and bow down to the ground before you?"

Honestly, I didn't know what it all meant. I just knew this is what I was dreaming. One day my brothers were tending to the flocks, and my father sent me to go see about them. Prior to leaving, my father had given me a beautiful coat of many colors. I put on my coat and was off to find my brothers. I went where my father told me to go at Shechem, but they were not there. I was told they went to Dothan, so off to Dothan I went.

As I was approaching my brothers, they spotted me and because of their jealousy and hatred toward me, they plotted to kill me. One of my brothers wanted to kill me by throwing me into the cisterns and saying that a ferocious animal devoured me. But Reuben said, "Let's not shed any blood, but let's toss him in a cistern here in the wilderness, but let's not lay a hand on him." When I got to my brothers, they stripped my coat off me and threw me in the cistern. It was empty and there was no water. Since the cistern was dry, they pulled me out and sold me to the Midianite merchants that were passing by. They sold me for a mere twenty shekels of silver.

They took my coat and smeared it with the blood of a slaughtered goat and took it back to my father and told him, "We found this. Examine it to see if it is your son's robe." It was then that my father, Jacob tore his clothes, put on sackcloth and mourned me for several days. All my other siblings went to him to comfort him, but he refused to be comforted.

I was taken to Egypt and by the favor of God, I lived in the house of the Egyptian master, Potiphar. Potiphar saw that the hand of the Lord was with me and I became his attendant. I was put in charge of his household, and he entrusted me with everything he owned.

Potiphar trusted me and I was loyal to him. However, one day my master's wife took notice of me and said, "Come to bed with me!" But I refused and responded to her by saying, "With me in charge, my master does not concern himself with anything in the house; everything he owns he has entrusted to my care. My master has withheld nothing from me except you, because you are his wife. How then could I do such a wicked thing and sin against God?"

When Grace & Mercy Met Me

She propositioned me several times, and each time I refused. There was this one particular day I was in the house attending to my duties and none of the servants were around, so she pulled on my cloak and said, "Come to bed with me!" But I denied her request and ran out the house and my cloak was still in her hand. When she realized she still had my cloak, she called her servant and said, "Look, my husband has brought this Hebrew slave here to make fools of us! He came into my room to rape me, but I screamed. When he heard me scream, he ran and got away, leaving his cloak behind." She waited until her husband got home and told him the same story, she told her servant.

Potiphar believed that I took advantage of his trust and had me put in prison. The favor of the Lord was upon me even in prison. Within time, the warden of the prison put me in charge over all the other prisoners and everything that happened in the prison.

I remember there were two prisoners that came, one was Pharaoh's chief cup-bearer and the other was his chief baker. One day each of them had a dream and wanted to know the meanings of their dreams. I realized something wasn't right with them, so I asked them what was wrong. They said, "We both had dreams last night, but no one can tell us what they mean."

They both shared their dreams with me. I told the cup-bearer that his dream represented that Pharaoh will come and reinstate him in his position in three days. As for the baker, his fate was not that of the baker. He, too, was released from prison, but his body would be impaled, placed on a pole and left for the birds to come peck away at his flesh. In three days both men were released from prison, and their fate was exactly as I had told them.

Two years later, Pharaoh had a series of dreams and it disturbed him that he didn't know what they meant. The cup-bearer spoke of a man that interrupted his dream while he was in prison, so Pharaoh sent for me to come at once. He told me his dream and I told him, "It's beyond my power to do this, but God can tell you what it means and set you at ease." The Lord showed me the meaning of Pharaoh's dream. Both of Pharaoh's dreams told of a series of good years the country would experience followed by seven years of famine. Pharaoh was thankful for the interpretation of the dream and took immediate action.

His actions resulted in Pharaoh appointing a supervisor of the land of Egypt to collect one-fifth of all crops to store during the good years so they will have enough food for all during the seven years of famine. It was at this time that Pharaoh appointed me as that supervisor.

See my gift made room for me. It took me out of prison and put me back in a position of authority that helped people. My motives were pure toward my assignment, and a hedge of protection was always with me. I didn't hold grudges against those that did wrong to me - my brothers, Potiphar's wife and others because I knew God was on my side. Just like I interrupted the dreams of others and they came true, I, too, was able to witness my own dreams coming forth just as they were given to me.

Just a little bit more to my story. The famine was vast and not only affected Egypt, but the surrounding areas as well, including Canaan, my homeland. I was the governor of all Egypt and I was in charge of selling grain, so everyone had to come to me to get grain. One day, my brothers came to get grain for their families. They came with their heads bowed, and they didn't recognize me, but I recognized them right away. I pretended to be a stranger and spoke harshly to them, "Where are you from?" They replied, "From the land of Canaan. We have come to buy food." I accused them of being spies and placed them in prison for three days. Then I said the only way to prove you are not spies is to go back to Canaan and bring me your youngest brother.

My brothers left to go back home. They were sent with a bag of grain and inside the money they had given, but when they returned with their brother, they returned the money that was placed back in their sack, along with additional money to buy more food. We had a feast, and there was a time in the evening when I had to step away and cry because I was overcome with emotion. Here I was with all my brothers, even Benjamin. I had also learned that my father was still alive. I wasn't ready to reveal my true identity yet, so I composed myself and returned to the festivities.

There is more to our story, and there was more back and forth for my brothers to and from Canaan. It finally got to be too much, and I finally revealed my true identity to my brothers. So now here I was, reunited with my family, all of my brothers as well as with my father. When I revealed myself to them, I told them not to be angry with themselves because it was part of God's plan. He had placed me in a position to help my family when help was needed. I told the story to Pharaoh, and he invited Jacob and the entire family to come live in Egypt.

See, those dreams that I had before my brothers sold me into slavery came true. I am thankful that God's protective hand was upon my life and that He allowed me to reunite with my family. Grace and mercy were extended to me to obtain favor with my masters and others who had rule over me. They all placed me in positions of power and authority because I was trustworthy. None of this would have been possible without God's grace and mercy and His ability to know the future before it happens. Even though I was rejected by my brothers, when the time came to help them, I did away with any heaviness and resentment and stepped right in helping them provide for the needs of my family. When they came to Egypt, they were treated with respect because of the power and authority God had bestowed upon me in that land.

When Grace & Mercy Met Me

They reaped the benefits of the protection the Lord had given to me.

My God-given gift to interpret dreams first caused me to be sold because of my brother's inability to see beyond self, but my gift was respected by the baker and Pharaoh. So, yes, my gift did save my life, not once but multiple times and not only for me, but for my family.

Don't allow the unknown to hinder you from walking in what you do know. If it is God ordained, it will all connect and make sense within time. I thank the Lord for His grace and mercy in my life.

As a young boy, I enjoyed working in the meadows tending to the sheep. My brothers didn't like it, but I loved being out there because it was so quiet. It gave me time to spend quality time with God. Being out there alone, I had to be brave and do some amazing things. I remember times when I was tending to the sheep and a bear or lion would come to take the sheep. I would have to strike them and retrieve the animal from its mouth. I have killed both lions and bears.

Everyone knows the story of when I, as a young lad, defeated the uncircumcised Philistine. Many had already tried to defeat him and couldn't, not even my older brothers. One day my father, Jesse, needed me to take some supplies to my brothers. They were in the army to defeat this giant. While I was down by my brothers, the Philistine came out and all the other men scattered in fear. I asked what shall be done to the man that kills the Philistine. My brothers didn't like the fact I was even there, but finally, I went to King Saul and said, "Let no man's heart fail because of him; thy servant will go and fight this Philistine."

Saul said to me, "You are not able to fight against this Philistine, for you are a child." I had to explain to him how I had to fight lions and bears in order to protect my father's sheep. I am qualified and I can do it. The Lord has been with me in the fields with the sheep, so I know He will be with me now. Finally, Saul agreed and gave me his armor to wear, but it was too big and heavy for me. I had to do this the way I knew how to do it. So, I chose five smooth stones from the brook and put them in my bag with the slingshot, and I was ready to go.

I headed out to fight the Philistine. He was confident that he could slay me because of my size and age, but I went into my bag, grabbed one of my stones and put it in my sling and got him right in his forehead. He fell to the ground. Once he was on the ground, I needed a sword to cut off his head, so I picked up the Philistine's sword and cut his head off with it. Saul was amazed at what was accomplished that day and he asked me, "Whose son are you?" I told him I am the son of Jesse the Bethlehemite.

Saul's son, Jonathan, and I became great friends and I stayed with Saul. Whatever mission he sent me out to do, I was successful, so he gave me a high rank in the army. My fellow soldiers were happy that I was there, but they began to sing, "Saul has slain his thousands, and David his tens of thousands." Saul didn't like that and got very jealous and began to watch me very closely. This was the beginning of Saul's fall.

An evil spirit from God had come upon Saul and when I played my harp, it soothed him. As I was playing my harp, Saul threw his spear at me, not once, but twice, and I was able to duck both times. Saul's attitude toward me changed, and it was evident that the hand of God was upon me and that He has been moved from Saul.

Even though Saul was at odds with me, he was still the king and I had to respect him. There were other times when he was trying to kill me, but I was able to avoid those attacks. There were times, too, where I had an opportunity to get back at him, but I chose not to because he was the king. God was protecting me. Finally, things got so bad with Saul that he became his own worst enemy and committed suicide by falling on his sword to avoid being captured in the battle against the Philistines at Mt. Gilboa.

Not too long after Saul's death, I was appointed the new king of Israel. I loved the Lord and was so thankful for the opportunity. He and I communed daily. When I was a young lad before I killed the giant, God had sent

When Grace & Mercy Met Me

Samuel to anoint me to be king one day, but even with the problems I was having with Saul, I knew it had to be in God's timing. The Lord testified concerning me saying, "I have found David, son of Jesse, a man after my own heart; he will do anything I want him to do." I had strong faith in God, and I surely needed it.

Even though God said I was a man after His own heart, it does not mean I never did wrong. Remember, I had an affair with Bathsheba, a married woman. To make matters worse, when we found out she was pregnant with my baby, I sent for Uriah, her husband, to come home so that he could have relations with her so no one would know that this was my baby. But being an honorable man, he refused to go home since the other soldiers were not able to go home. So, for his nobility, I sent him back to the war with a letter to his commander telling him to send Uriah to the battle frontlines. Do you see how wrong I was in this story? Now as a king, I had blood on my hands. Blood of an innocent man.

My life was full in those 40 years of being the king of Israel. I had both ups and downs during my reign. As I look back over my life, I really see where the Lord had His hand upon me. I want to boldly thank the Lord for His protection in my life. He has covered me for my entire life, and I want to thank Him for His grace and mercy. I received such favor in my life that I didn't deserve or that He kept from the things I truly deserved.

When Grace & Mercy Met Me

If I had to do it all over again, I would still serve Him as I served Him, but I would work on being more conscious of my actions and behaviors and do things differently. I don't like to share stories about my life. I am not happy about all the bloodshed as a result of my command. The situation with Uriah was not necessary because I was covering my own issues by taking the life of someone else.

Lord, I repent of my actions and thank you that I have the opportunity to spend eternity with you in heaven because despite my downfalls, you still prevailed in my life. Despite my pitfalls, you provided your grace and mercy to me. I am eternally thankful! Thank you, Lord!

ALL OF YOU HAVE SHARED YOUR STORIES of God's grace and mercy. Well, I, too, have a story to share. I was living a life of sin. I was a prostitute, and everyone knew it. I was young, beautiful, always with a big smile and knew how to gain attention. I was often enticed by my admirers when they showered me with gifts of silver and gold. I was determined to get as much of it as I could.

I remember the day I met Hosea. He came to me and boldly proclaimed, "The Lord has commanded me to marry you. You shall become my wife, and we shall have children." I wasn't sure why God had told this man to marry me; after all, I was a harlot and he was a prophet of God. He was God's mouthpiece, so I was perplexed, but Hosea was confident in what he proclaimed. Everyone knew who we both were, so why had God chosen this union?

I accepted Hosea's proposal and we did marry, but it was difficult for me to give up the lifestyle I lived, so I committed adultery against my husband.

Historians have related my marriage to Hosea to symbolize God's covenant relationship with Israel. The Lord used Hosea to tell the story of Israel's disobedience, His discipline and steadfastness, and His faithful love for Israel. The rejection and betrayal shown by Israel resembled me leaving a good home with a good, God-fearing husband to go out in the streets for other men. But for Israel, they left God to worship idols.

I remember one night when I saw a man hurrying toward me and as he got closer, it was Hosea. He yelled to me, saying, "Gomer, come home." I reluctantly obliged him and came home. God gave me a good man, but good can sometimes be tiresome and boring. As he continued to speak of God and faithfulness to covenant, my spirit was often dampened, and he made me to feel ashamed of my sins. I couldn't understand how I could be so wrong to dream of having a little pleasure in this life.

I now realize how I hurt my husband over and over. Each time he had to come out and find me, it broke his heart. If I had only stopped for a moment to listen to my husband's heart, I would have seen that I had broken it time and time again. What I really didn't know or realize was that it was difficult for my husband to even marry me when he did. God instructed him, saying, "Go marry a promiscuous wife and have children with her." The life I continued to live after my marriage to Hosea was representative of how Israel rejected God. I have come to realize that each time my husband went out to find me and bring me home, he was restoring and bringing reconciliation back to our marriage. The actions of my husband and his love for me were the same actions of God had toward Israel and His love for that nation.

The things my husband endured at my misconduct were extreme; however, the message Hosea had to deliver to the people of Israel was harsh. He did it in a tender way while being heartbroken.

I am so grateful for the grace and mercy God granted me for giving me my husband. If I would have known then what I know now, I would have stayed home and made a home for my husband and children. I would have been there to support my husband and pray for him and encourage him when he struggled with the Word of the Lord that he had to deliver to Israel to warn them. I would have been a loving wife and a homemaker instead of continuing to run out to the streets and live the life of sin. Lord, I thank you for your grace and mercy!

I HAVE A TESTIMONY, I didn't like the assignment given to me, so I decided to run from God and the assignment. The message of doom that I had to tell the people annoyed me, and I just couldn't get things together to tell them. I was God's mouthpiece to share those things He shared with me for the people, but I ran. I already knew the end result, so that is what kept me from doing what I was called to do. Even while on the run from God's plans and desires for my life, He spared my life.

Let me back up a little and tell you my story. The Lord spoke to me saying, "Go to Nineveh and preach and tell of the doom that is coming in 40 days, because its wickedness has come before me." I questioned to commands because how was I supposed to go bring this word? What would they do to me? I dismissed God's command and went my own direction. I believed that I could run from the Lord and His command, so I paid my fare and boarded a ship to Tarshish.

That night the winds became great and a violent storm arose which threatened the safety of all those on the ship. The sailors were fearful and began to throw cargo overboard to make the ship lighter. While all this was happening, I was fast asleep below deck. The captain came to let me know what was going on and was amazed that I was sleeping while all the calamity was occurring.

The crew began to realize that there was something different about this storm and that it must be some type of punishment for someone aboard. So, they cast lots to find out who was responsible for this calamity. All signs pointed to me, so they began to question me. "Tell us, who is responsible for making all this trouble for us? What kind of work do you do? Where do you come from? What is your country? From what people are you?" I responded by telling them that I was a Hebrew and I worship the Lord, the God of heaven, who made the sea and the dry land.

As I was speaking, they became nervous and asked me, "What have you done?" They knew I was running from the Lord, and the sea began to get rougher and rougher. They thought I had the solution to make the sea calm down, so they asked what they should do. I told them, "Pick me up and throw me into the sea, and it shall become calm."

As I reflect back, this was just another way I was trying to escape my assignment. Now my running was harming others, so it was best for me to be tossed into the sea. I knew it was my fault that they were experiencing this storm. I was willing to die by being tossed into the sea to evade my assignment from the Lord.

Even though everyone understood what we were now facing, the men could not throw me overboard. They did all they could to row us back to land, but the sea would not give up. The waves grew even stronger, so they began to cry out to the Lord by saying, "Please, Lord do not let us die for taking this man's life. Do not hold us accountable for killing an innocent man." It is then that they regrettably threw me overboard.

As I was tossed into the sea, the Lord provided a huge fish to swallow me up. I was in the belly of this fish for three long days and nights. As I entered the fish, I began to pray. As I was in the belly of the fish, I cried out to the Lord for forgiveness. I began to see my wrongs, and my heart hurt because I knew I wasn't doing what God told me to do. It was at this time I entered in to worship and offered him praises of thanksgiving. My heart was heavy due to my disobedience and I being a mouthpiece of God, not only affected my walk with Him but also affected those whose life was assigned to me through the message I had to deliver. I was remorseful of my actions. With seaweed wrapped all around my head, I declared that, "Salvation comes from the Lord." I cried and cried, but the Lord heard me and spoke to the fish, and it vomited me out onto the seashore. I was on dry land. I laid there and wept, but the Lord began to speak to me. He said, "Get up and go, go to Nineveh and preach to them. Proclaim the message I gave to you because they are in a bad way and I can no longer ignore it."

I set out to Nineveh and I was determined to obey God's command, word for word not deviating from it at all. Nineveh was a very large city and it took me three days to walk from one side to the place I needed to share the word of the Lord.

The people gathered to hear what I, the prophet of God, had to share with them. I proclaimed a warning to the people, "In forty days Nineveh will be overtaken." Their belief in God was strong, and they immediately declared a citywide fast. The city demonstrated such unity because everyone participated in this fast, all from the rich and poor, the famous and commoners, leaders and followers, even the animals.

The king gave a decree, "Do not let people or animals, herds, flocks, taste anything. Do not let them eat or drink." He continued by saying, "Dress them all in sackcloth and worship the Lord by crying out to Him for help. We must all turn from our evil ways and no longer allow the violent ways that have stained our hands no longer control our ways. Cry out and ask the

When Grace & Mercy Met Me

Lord to have compassion on us and turn us from evil so that we shall not perish."

The Lord heard their prayers and changed His mind and destruction did not threaten them. It was their display of unity and how they exercised their faith as one. One would think that this would have made me happy and satisfied and thankful for this experience. One would think that I would reflect back about being in the belly of the fish, which I did not like, but that I would be thankful and would have had a change of heart. After all, I was obedient and through my obedience, thousands of people's lives were saved from destruction and through my obedience the people's faith in God increased. These are all great things and a good reason to be happy and thankful, but why did I get so angry?

I remember getting furious with God yelling at him, "I knew this was going to happen. That is why I fled to Tarshish. I had to go through all that I went through despite you still showing your grace and mercy to this evil city. I just don't get it."

I was so angry. I continued to let Him know all that was in my mind. I spewed all my anger toward God with several questions. I cried out saying, "I didn't understand why You saved Nineveh because their nation is at war with Israel, so by it being destroyed, Israel would have gained a victory. God, they don't deserve Your judgment because of the evil they had done and You made me look like I didn't know what I was talking about. You had me to go and tell them they were going to be destroyed, but instead, You saved them. Why did you need me? I just don't understand. Nineveh needs to be punished. I knew this was going to happen, that's why I didn't want to do it. This just makes no sense. So, if you won't kill them, kill me! I'm better off dead!"

Then the Lord spoke to me saying, "What do you have to be angry about?" I was still so angry that I went out and built a makeshift shelter and sat there rehashing the situation over and over stewing in my anger.

As I sat there a leafed tree sprung up to give me shade. The presence of the tree took my mind off my anger and actually made me happy. The next morning when I woke, the tree was gone, worms had come and ate the tree overnight and it died. It was a hot day and I really needed that shade, so I became angry again and prayed, "I'm better off dead!"

Now God came back to me saying, "What right do you have to get angry about this shade tree?" He continued by saying, "How is it that you can change your feelings from pleasure to anger overnight about this tree that you did nothing to get? You didn't water it, nor did you plant it. It grew up one night and died the next. So, if you can change your feelings about the tree, why can't I change my feelings about Nineveh from anger to pleasure? Nineveh is a large city with more than 120,000 childlike people who have to learn to grow in me. They don't know right from wrong, so they have to learn. I know that the Ninevites learned their lesson and have changed their direction."

Once the Lord explained this to me, I began to better understand the lesson He was sharing with me. I just had to walk in my obedience no matter what the outcome was. I failed to see that it's the way of the Lord, not mine. I overreacted and once I did my part, I should have been done. All the anger and spewing was pointless; however, it did show me, me. I began to see the message in this for myself. By being a mouthpiece for the Lord, my mouth and heart were not aligned. I began to realize that there are things in my heart that need to be removed so that I can serve Him without doubt and without my own agenda. I began to ask myself, "How can I be my mouthpiece and then get angry when things don't go your way."

I began to realize that the same grace and mercy that the Lord gave to the city of Nineveh is the same grace and mercy He gave me. I was looking at Nineveh's sin, yet overlooking my own. If I would have known then what I know now, I would have stayed in Nineveh and rejoiced with them over the Lord sparing them. But now I rejoice because He has also spared me.

A Mother's Love

MY NAME WAS NEVER MENTIONED IN THE BIBLE, but I know the story made it. I have so much to be thankful for because of the situation I faced. Let me start by saying, "A mother knows her child, and I knew that baby I found lying next to me was not my son."

My friend and I lived together. I had my baby and then three days later she had hers. We loved our babies, but one night while she was sleeping, she rolled over and her son died. She was devastated and didn't know what to do, but then she did the imaginable. She came into my room and switched my son with her son's dead body. I couldn't figure out why or how she could do such a thing. Didn't she know I would figure it out?

WHEN GRACE & MERCY MET ME

When I woke up and realized what had happened, I was devastated and went to her immediately. I asked her to give me my baby back, but she insisted that I already had my baby.

She and I got into an argument because I knew that the baby that was alive was my son. His smile and movements were sketched in my heart, so I just knew he was mine. She would not back down, so we had to take our misunderstanding to a mediator: the king.

We explained the situation to King Solomon and another argument erupted between us, and finally the King hushed us and spoke by saying, "Bring me a sword." He said, "I have a solution," then he made the order, "Cut the baby in half! That way each of you will have a part of him." Immediately, my heart sank. I couldn't let this happen to my son. I just couldn't. I cried out to the king saying, "Please don't kill my son. I love him so much, but give him to her, but please just don't kill him."

As I was crying and begging the king to give him to her, she started saying, "Go ahead and cut him in half. Then neither of us will have the baby." What was she saying? She was not speaking clearly nor was she thinking clearly. What if the roles were reversed? Would she be saying those same things? My spirit was crushed, but I had to fight for my son. He was born of my flesh, and I just had to fight for him.

Solomon heard our pleas and made his decree. He said, "Don't kill the baby." As he looked at me and handed me my son, he said, "I know that you are the real mother because of your willingness to let her have him to save his life. Only the real mother would do such a noble thing."

I am so grateful and thankful for the wisdom God had given Solomon.

The lesson I learned on that day is that when we are right and we stand our ground, the Lord will show Himself strong in our lives. He will give us a testimony to share that will point back to His grace and mercy that is available to us daily. I didn't know I had the strength I possessed until I had to go through this situation. I am just so thankful for the Lord being on my side and fighting for me through the wisdom the king had.

Like I said earlier, a mother knows her child and nothing can come between the bond they share. I just knew that was my baby.

Mary, Jesus' Mother

NO ONE REALLY PAID ANY ATTENTION TO ME. I was born to a poor family that lived in Nazareth. I didn't do anything spectacular to draw attention, and my friends probably wouldn't vote me most likely to succeed. However, I did meet a wonderful man, and we were engaged to be married. He was very kind to me, and I loved him so much.

I stayed to myself a lot and maintained a small circle. I remember this day so clearly. I was just going about my business and suddenly, he appeared, an angel. He greeted me by saying, "Greetings, favored one!" I thought, favored one, what does that mean? The angel proceeded to say, "The Lord is with you, do not be afraid, you have found favor with God." I stood in amazement as I listened to the words coming forth. I had heard the stories of the coming Messiah, so what the angel was telling me wasn't anything new, except for the part when he told me that I would be the one to conceive and give birth as a virgin to the Son of God.

What? I am the chosen vessel for the Lord and Savior to come forth? I felt so honored and eagerly accepted this assignment. I submitted to becoming pregnant by the Holy Spirit.

I knew by saying yes that I would face some hard times. I knew people would talk badly about me and think that Joseph and I had come together before our wedding day. I also knew that God could comfort and keep me strong while enduring all these rumors and accusations. I also knew that Joseph would be right by my side, especially after I learned that the angel also visited him and explained it to him. Joseph was very supportive.

We can do this!

Raising Jesus and knowing that He was God's seed was an amazing experience. It was hard to get upset with Him, but we did and we still loved Him immensely. I can remember the time when He was 12 years old and got separated from us. We thought He was with us. We had traveled a day's journey back home before realizing He had stayed in Jerusalem. We had to turn around and travel another day's journey just to go and search for Him. When we finally found Him, He was at the temple among the teachers listening and asking questions. Both His questions and His answers were amazing the elders He was conversing with. His wisdom was way beyond His age.

When I finally found Him, I went to Him and said, "Son, what are you doing? Your father and I have been looking for you. You were supposed to be with us, and now we had to turn back to locate you." My dear son Jesus innocently and boldly responded, "I had to be about my Father's business."

When He spoke those words to us, we had no clue what He was saying. We just gathered Him up and returned home to Nazareth.

My son was always doing spectacular things. His father Joseph missed many of the things because he passed away before Jesus really began His ministry. Joseph was very proud of our son.

I remember being at a wedding in Cana, and my son performed a miracle right before our eyes. The wine ran dry, so He ordered the servants to fill containers with water and to draw out some and take it to the chef. When the chef tasted it, he said to the groom, "You saved the best of the wine for last." He had no clue of what my son just did.

Jesus was always teaching, imparting wisdom and sharing with those around Him. His presence drew crowds. I tried to be with Him when it was possible. I was a proud mother, and I loved my son.

When Grace & Mercy Met Me

He loved me also. I heard news that my son was arrested and that He was being taken to Golgotha. John, Ruth, Jude and I arrived just as He was being hoisted to His position on the cross. The sight of Him was so horrific; the images are still stuck in my mind. He saw me and yelled to His brother John saying, "I desire that you depart from this place." So, John took us away.

I saw the power that radiated from Him while being on that cross and knew that it was to complete the work of His Heavenly Father, but that was my son. I yearned to be there for Him. Yes, I remember the scriptures of old, but the reality of it was a bit overwhelming.

After Passover, I returned to Bethsaida with my son John and lived with him. Life was different without the flesh and blood of my son Jesus; however, His blood was still alive. It's alive right now and He's interceding for us all. His blood was given sacrificially so that we all can live.

I'm thankful to the Heavenly Father for the pure honor to serve in the way He allowed me to serve and bring the life of His beloved son into the earth. I received an extension of grace and mercy because of the favor God said I obtained while a young girl. My son, Jesus, was unique and without sin. I love my boy, and I know I will see Him again.

Martha

WHY IS IT THAT THE OLDER SISTER ALWAYS has to do all the work? I had invited Jesus and His disciples over and since it was about mealtime, I decided to make them something to eat. Jesus has been to our home many times and is a good friend of ours, but I don't understand why Mary just sat at His feet while I raced around trying to get everything in order. I'd call for her to come and assist me, but she ignored my requests and just sat at His feet and hung on every word He spoke.

As I was running around getting everything together for our guests, I remember coming out and asking Jesus, "Lord, do You not care that my sister has left me to serve alone? Therefore, tell her to help me." I didn't get the response from Him that I expected. He softly said, "Martha, Martha, you are worried and troubled about many things, but one thing is needed and Mary has chosen that good part, which will not be taken away from her."

He took my sister's side. I wasn't happy about that, but continued to go and prepare the meal for our guests. As I worked, I began to wonder what the good part was that Jesus spoke of. Dinner was finally served, and once I had an opportunity to sit with the others and enjoy the meal, Jesus continued to speak and I finally realized what He meant.

Once I paid attention, my understanding was enlightened. We all have choices and we have to respect the choices of others. We can't expect them to do as we would do, but we need to respect their choices. Jesus tells us that our highest priority is to seek first the kingdom of God and His righteousness, and then all these things shall be added to you. We can't put ourselves and our agendas before the will of God. I realized that Mary chose to sit and listen to the wisdom of Jesus while she had the opportunity, while I chose to run around and fuss.

I see where my sister wasn't wrong in her actions and wish I would have realized it sooner. If I would have known what was really happening, I, too, would have sat more and listened to what He was sharing. I'm thankful that when I allowed my view of the situation overtake me enough to go and whine that He was

When Grace & Mercy Met Me

gentle with me. He showed His grace and mercy to me even though I was in the wrong.

Sometime later our brother Lazarus had gotten extremely ill and he died. We sent for Jesus to come before our brother died, but Lazarus was dead for four days before Jesus could get to him. As we waited for Him to come to our brother's rescue, we started to get weary and outright upset because it was taking Him so long. We called for Him to come, but He stayed in Bethany two extra days. Did He not care about His friends? When He finally arrived, Jesus was moved to tears and it pained Him to see the anguish Mary and I were experiencing over our brother's death. Through it all, He was still able to raise our brother from the grave. He said He had to bring him back to life because of the pain He saw us in. All we could do was rejoice because our brother was no longer dead.

All four of us were good friends and Jesus had even been a guest in our home several times. He knew us very well and loved us very much. Even though we may have been a little upset with Him, all was forgiven once our brother was alive and well. The joy we had over the miracle we witnessed erased all the feelings of anger and animosity we started to have. I realize that it was our faith becoming weary that allowed us to become angry and uptight.

Now for a second time, Jesus gave me a reason and opportunity to learn from Him. Again, we cannot have things done in our timing and what we expect, but we have to trust God's timing. He knew our feelings, yet He did not rebuke us; instead, He performed a miracle on our behalf. He brought our brother back to life. Again, He handled the situation with such grace while offering us His grace and mercy.

Now I must do better. I have learned to not doubt Him one bit. If He said it, I know He will do it. I don't fuss at my sister because I know she is receiving the things she needs, and I have learned to respect her choices as well as the choices of others.

I HAD THE HONOR AND PLEASURE to be with Jesus Himself. He chose me. I had just gotten onto the shore from an unsuccessful overnight fishing trip. My team and I were cleaning up and getting the boat prepared for when we ventured out the next day. As we were working, Jesus got on the boat and asked us to row out from the shore. As we went out into the waters, Jesus preached to the crowd. When He finished, He instructed me, saying, "Row the boat out into the deep, let down your nets so you can catch some fish." I responded to Him saying, "Master, we have worked hard all night and caught nothing, but since you tell me to do so, I will go into the deep and let down the nets." So that's what my team and I did. Guess what? We witnessed a miracle, and our labors were not in vain.

WHEN GRACE & MERCY MET ME

We caught an abundance of fish, so much that our nets began to rip apart. We couldn't handle it all on our own, so we had to signal for our partners to come in their boats to help us gather our catch. Can you believe it, both boats were so full that they both began to sink? I had great gratitude in my heart for what Jesus had done for my business and compelled to just drop to my knees and confess by saying, "Lord, don't come near me! I am a sinner." It was then that Jesus assured me to not be afraid and said, "From now on, you will bring in people instead of fish; you will be fishers of men." He then spoke to us; James, John and myself and said, "If anyone would come after me, let him deny himself and take up your cross and follow me." We left our professions and chose to follow Him.

He selected twelve men to be discipled and taught by Him personally. During our time with Jesus, we received very rich teachings, witnessed so many miracles, and traveled across the land. Being part of His inner circle along with Andrew, James and John, we saw so much that we just can't speak of it all. I do remember one day Jesus took us up to the mountain to pray and as He was praying, His appearance began to change. His face shined like the sun, and His clothes became as white as the light; then all of a sudden, there appeared Moses and Elijah speaking with Jesus. They were speaking about His departure and the purpose as to why He came to the earth to fulfill while here. I wasn't sure exactly what had happened or if I was even supposed to witness this, so I asked Jesus, "Lord, is it good for us to be here?" As I was speaking, a bright cloud covered us and we heard a voice from the cloud say, "This is my Son, whom I love; with Him I am well pleased. Listen to Him!" I'm not even going to lie. We got scared and fell facedown to the ground, but Jesus comforted us by touching us saying, "Get up, don't be afraid," and when we stood up all we saw was Jesus. The others were gone. Jesus said to us, "Do not tell anyone what you had seen until after I have been risen from the dead."

One day we were all traveling from Bethsaida to Caesarea Philippi. We stopped to rest and Jesus asked us, "Who do men say that I am?" I remember someone answering, "Some say you are John the Baptist." Another responded by saying, "Some believe you are the Prophet Elijah or Prophet Jeremiah." He listened to our responses, then He asked, "But what about you? Who do you say that I am?" Immediately I responded and said, "You are the Messiah, the Son of the living God." This answer astonished Jesus and He replied by saying, "Blessed are you Simon for this was not revealed to you by flesh and blood, but by my Father in heaven." I knew He was different than any other man I have ever met, and it was through the revelation of God Himself that He showed Himself to me through His Son, Jesus who was my Master and Teacher.

I have to share this other phenomenal memory I have being with our Lord. I remember He just got done teaching to the crowds and as He dismissed the crowds, and the disciples got on the boat. We thought that He, too, came to the boat after dismissing the crowds, so we started our way across to the other side. Instead, Jesus had gone on the mountainside to pray by Himself. When He returned to the shore, He was there alone, and the boat was already a considerable distance from the land. It was just after dawn, and we looked out and saw Jesus walking toward us. He was walking on the water. At first several of us thought it was a ghost coming toward us and fear set in. Jesus saw the fear we possessed and said to us, "Take courage! It is I; don't be afraid." I responded back by asking, "Lord, if it's you, tell me to come to you on the water," then Jesus said, "Come." With a mixture of eagerness and excitement, I got down out of the boat, and I began to walk on the water and was heading right toward Jesus. Everything was great when I was looking straight ahead and focusing on where I wanted to go, but I took a quick glimpse at my surroundings and it quickly set in. I was walking on water! It was at that moment when I saw the wind, and the fear of sinking entered my mind and I cried out, "Lord, save me!" I stepped out of the boat having great faith, but once I took my eyes off Jesus, fear overtook me. Jesus reached out His hand and caught me, then He said, "You of little faith, why did you doubt?" Once we got back in the boat, the winds died down and the other disciples who witnessed this event began to worship Him, saying, "Truly you are the Son of God."

I loved Jesus and would do anything for Him. The day came when Jesus prepared for us a meal and shared with us the weight of His fate. He said to us, "I have eagerly desired to eat this Passover with you before I suffer. This is my last meal before I fulfill the kingdom of God." He took the cup and gave thanks and said, "Take this and divide it among you." Then He took the bread, gave thanks and broke it and instructed us again to take a piece of the bread. As we were taking the bread, He said, "This is my body given to you; do this in remembrance of me. This cup is the new covenant in my blood, which is poured out for you." We all listened intently. Then He said, "The hand of him who is going to betray me is with us now at the table." Everyone began to look around and we began to question who the betrayer was. We proceeded with our supper.

After supper there was a time that Jesus and I were alone, and He began to warn me and encourage me. He shared with me that it was Satan's desire to sift me as wheat, but He told me to not let my faith fail me. I expressed my gratitude with Him and said, "Lord, I am ready to go with you both to prison and to death." Jesus quickly stopped me and said, "I tell you, Peter, the rooster will not crow this day, until you deny three times that you know me."

Shortly after this conversation, Jesus and I, along with a few other disciples, went to the Mount of Olives to pray. We were to stay and watch while He went and prayed, but it was late and we were tired and fell asleep. Jesus came and woke us and said, "Why are you sleeping? Rise and pray that you may not enter into temptation." He had blood on His face and all over His body, when we looked at Him, it looked as though He was sweating blood.

When Grace & Mercy Met Me

As we were speaking, a crowd of people came and was being led by Judas. Judas drew near to Jesus and kissed Him. It was then that some from the crowd grabbed Jesus to arrest Him. I acted on my impulse to help, and I drew my sword and cut the ear off the high priest's servant. Jesus quickly rebuked me by saying, "No more of this." Then He touched the man's ear and healed him. The rest of the evening was a blur. They took Jesus and the ones that were with Him fled. As I was seen by some, they pointed out that I was one of His followers, and I would deny that they were correct. This happened three times and finally after the third time, the rooster crowed and I feel to my knees and wept. I felt such shame. I just confessed to going to prison for Him and to death for Him, yet I denied Him and turned away from Him at a time when He needed us the most. I was truly crushed.

He was taken back and forth, and finally His fate was given to Him. He was to be crucified on a cross like He was a criminal. He was wrongly accused of so much, but through all of the allegations, He remained humble and was still able to teach from His position on the cross. One of the thieves that was hung next Him watched and observed and realized that Jesus was an innocent man. Jesus cried out and said, "Father, forgive them, for they do not know what they are doing." Then this other man hanging on the cross next to Jesus rebuked the crowd saying, "Don't you fear God? This other man and I have been punished justly, for we are getting what our deeds deserve, but this man between us has done nothing wrong." Then he looked over to

When Grace & Mercy Met Me

Jesus and said, "Jesus, please remember me when you come into your kingdom." Jesus replied and said, "Truly, I tell you, today you will be with me in paradise."

The sky turned dark and Jesus called out with a loud voice, "Father, into your hands I commit my spirit." He then breathed His last breath, Jesus was died. My heart hurt so much because I let Him down. He went and defeated the devil in Hell. He went to hell for all the sins of this world even though He was without sin.

The next time I saw Jesus was while we were by the Sea of Galilee. A few others and I went out to fish, but we caught nothing. Early that morning, Jesus stood on the shore, but we did not recognize Him. He called out to us, "Friends, don't you have any fish?" Someone from our group responded and said, "No." Then He said, "Throw your net on the right side of the boat and you will find fish." We did so and our nets were bursting with fish. It was at this moment that I recognized who had been speaking to us. I turned to Him with great zeal and excitement and said, "It is the Lord! It is the Lord!" I immediately jumped into the water and ran to Jesus. It was so good to see Him. Everything happened to Him just like He shared with us at the last supper; He died, went to hell, defeated Satan, rose again and now He possessed the keys to the Kingdom.

Jesus and I sat and talked for a while and He asked me three times, "Peter, do you love me?" Each time I answered, "Yes, Lord, you know that I love you." Each time I would respond, He would respond by saying things like, "Feed my lambs. Take care of my sheep!"

As time went on, I heard the stories of how He was looking for His disciples. I heard stories that He asked for me by name. Why was it that Jesus, who died to save all of creation, was now looking for me specifically? I had denied Him and was no use to Him when He was in His greatest need. As I reflect back, He was preparing me for my assignment. He knew what was in me. All that forwardness I possessed while He was teaching us was just waiting to be used to give Him glory. I had to go through these times of despair to finally realize what it was He wanted me to do. So, when the day of Pentecost came and with the power of the Holy Spirit burning on the inside of me, I could speak with boldness and tell the people, "Repent and be baptized every one of you in the name of Jesus Christ for the remission of sins, and you shall receive the gift of the Holy Spirit." That day over 3000 people came to love the one that I loved so much.

Despite my little faith on the water, my anger in the garden and my denial of Jesus, I was still a vessel God could use. His grace and mercy were made available to me, He knew what was within me and I stepped up to fulfill the purpose God had for me.

WHEW, DO I HAVE A TESTIMONY to share with you. I can't share it all because it will take pages and pages, volumes and volumes. You can read in detail about my story and the messages God gave me in thirteen books of the New Testament, but today I'd like to take the time to share some of the high points.

I am not a boastful man, but I do believe that the work God did in me is still affecting those in today's generation because of the great revelations He entrusted me with. Millions of people have the opportunity to read the Word of God, but I just shared what He gave me.

Let me share about my life from a first-hand aspect. I was born Saul of Tarsus to Jewish parents who possessed Roman citizenship. I began studying the

When Grace & Mercy Met Me

Hebrew Scriptures under the leadership of Rabbi Gamaliel in the city of Jerusalem, and it was through him that I began an in-depth study of the Law. Rabbi Gamaliel was the leading authority of the Sanhedrin, and it was through his teachings too that I earned a high ranking within the council, and it was through this counsel that we were punishing people for not obeying the law. We were also persecuting Christians for their belief in Christ and sentencing them to death because as a Pharisee, we did not believe in the resurrection of Christ.

I remember I was on my way to Damascus to seek out and arrest followers of Jesus. The purpose of the trip was to return to Jerusalem with prisoners to question them and possibly execute them, but my journey was interrupted when I saw a bright light, it was so bright that it blinded me. Not only was there this great light that caused me to fall to the ground, but I also heard a divine voice that communicated directly to me by saying, "Saul, Saul, why do you persecute me?" I responded to the voice by saying, "Who are you, Lord?" The voice answered by saying, "I am Jesus, whom you are persecuting. Now get up and go into the city and you will be told what you must do." Those that were with me were astonished and could not speak. When I was finally ready to get up, I got up from the ground, but I could not see once I opened my eyes. I had to be led by hand into Damascus, and for three days I was blind and did not eat or drink anything.

When Grace & Mercy Met Me

This was the day my life changed forever. My physical sight was compromised, but my spiritual sight was enlightened. I gained a great understanding for who Jesus was and what His purpose was. It was through my conversion that I learned just how wrong I was all these years to not believe who Jesus was. After this day, I knew He was truly the son of God. I came to know Him as the resurrected savior to all mankind. So, just as I was dedicated to my beliefs while I was Saul the Pharisee, I now was dedicated to my beliefs as Paul, the Apostle of the Lord Jesus Christ. I quickly learned that it is in Him that we live and move and have our very existence. I also learned that for me to live is Christ and to die is gain.

I was an apostle appointed by God. He sent me out to share the good news of the gospel to the Gentiles. Going out and preaching the good news was not an easy job, I had to gain the trust of people because after all I was Saul the Pharisee who persecuted Christians for their beliefs, and now I am telling them of the grace and mercy God has given them. The Lord dealt with me on numerous topics that I was to share with the churches. He directed my steps on where to go and share His Word. As He sent me out to the churches in the land to tell of His goodness, the false teachers (Pharisees) would go behind me to discourage the people and try hard to discredit the word I shared with them and who I truly was. This is why I had to write letters to the various churches to reiterate what I had taught to them while there in person and to warn them of what was happening. I knew confusion was being stirred up, and I had to bring comfort and understanding to them through my letters.

I personally faced so many trials and tribulations to do my assignment for the Lord. I was beaten and left for dead many times, I was wrongly accused and put in prison, I was stoned and so much more. But it was through these trials that I gained my strength. Everything I experienced; I know Jesus experienced much worse. It was in my times of weakness that I saw just how strong I was and how much He was with me. I gained strength in my weakness. Strength in the Spirit.

All I knew is that I had been given grace and mercy for the wrongs of my past, the blood that was on my hands has been forgiven by the blood of Jesus. The many sacrifices I made were not even enough to make up for all the love He has given to me. I am eternally thankful for His grace and mercy and the pure honor it was to serve Him in the capacity that He called me to. As mentioned before, I am not a boastful man regarding my own works, but I will boast all day about the goodness of the Lord Jesus Christ, my Lord and Savior! My life was never the same, and for that I am grateful!

Jesus

MY DEAR BROTHERS AND SISTERS. Our Father sent me so that we all may have a great and abundant life. He has loved you since the time He created Adam and Eve and placed them in the Garden of Eden. When He created them, you were also on His mind. When He made the promise to Abraham that he would be the father of many nations, you were also on His mind. He has never stopped thinking of you. I was there with Him during all the planning.

As He looked down upon the earth and saw the struggles, He knew He needed to send His righteousness to the earth. Me being one with Him is the reason why He chose that I come be the sacrificial lamb to save all of mankind. See when Adam first sinned, the process of death and sacrificial giving began. God had to kill an animal to clothe Adam and Eve now that they had eaten from the tree of good and evil, they realized they were naked.

Eve, I want you to know that despite being deceived by the serpent, God still loves you and forgives you.

Cain, you were right. Our Heavenly Father did have His hand of protection on you despite the wrongs you did to your brother. He realized what had happened and knew that eventually you would become remorseful of your ways and learn from your mistakes.

Sarah, you and Abraham encountered a lot of laughter at the promise God had for you, but He had the last laugh. He came through with everything He promised you. That's just how He is. He never disappoints.

Ham, yes, you were part of the group that was saved to replenish the earth. The actions you did, yes, they were wrong, but I'm here to remind you that God still loves you.

Ma'am, you and your husband Lot had a lot going on. The ways of this world distracted you and drew you away from my Father's presence and law. You suffered the consequences of your decision; however, with all that, God still loves you.

Joseph, I had to put you in position. Even though what happened to you didn't seem right, it worked out for your good. You were blessed with a powerful gift of interpreting dreams and when you spoke about your gift saved you, it was such a profound statement. Our Father was pleased when He heard you speak of your gifts in such a way.

David, despite all your calamity and the bloodshed from your orders, you still were a man after Our Father's heart. You knew how to take ownership of the wrongs you did and pray to Him for forgiveness and through repentance. I am glad to call you brother.

Gomer, as you have come to know, God had a plan for you and your life. It doesn't matter what you did before. What matters is that He captured your attention to realize what it is He needed of you.

Jonah, I am thankful that you saw things the way of the Father and ended up rejoicing for the people of Nineveh. You were trying to be the one in control, but you must always remember, God is in complete control and we must yield to Him. Your turn around was great and I was cheering for you to come around and see things as the Father saw them...and you did! Right on!

Young lady, I honor you for being upright and showing the tenacity to fight for your child. Children come into this world innocent and it is the job of the parents to nurture them, to love them and to provide for them, as well as, fight for them when something wrong has been done to them. Your child being taken from you was something wrong, but you truly filled the role of being a protective mother for your child. God is well pleased with you.

Mother, or as others call you, Mary; thank you for your yes! I know it may have been difficult raising me because I was so focused on fulfilling the will of my Heavenly Father that sometimes I worried you and my father Joseph. You were an amazing mother, and the strength within you was seen by many. I love you and so does our Heavenly Father. Thank you for your life that gave me life.

Martha, Martha, Martha! When I was at your house and you were fussing, you were such a sight. All I can honestly say is that you truly caught on to what it was you were doing and you made an immediate change. You took heed to the few words I spoke and grew from it. Your growth in that moment was amazing and I recognized it immediately as well.

Peter, we had some experiences. Whew did we ever. The more time we spent together, your temperament calmed and you were able to walk in the full power and authority I had given you. When I walked the earth, people were healed by their faith to just touch my garments and then as you matured, people were healed by your very shadow. The road was rocky, but we made it. I just want you to know I love you and so does our Father in Heaven. I love you, bro!

Paul, the work you did was astonishing. The Father and I knew it was there all along. We just had to get your attention. You decreased yourself and became a conduit from which the revelations flowed in order to bring as many to Christ as possible. You knew that Jewish Law inside out and backwards, but once you understood Christianity, you did away with the Jewish Law. You realized that so much more was being added to it than Our Father originally intended. You suffered, but like you told others, I will tell you; your suffering was not in vain. There is a purpose behind all things concerning Our Father.

To the many others in the good book, the Bible that were not mentioned; people such as King Saul, Queen Ester, Deborah, Sampson, Elijah, and the many more that could have had their stories shared God loves all of His creation. He loves every man, woman and child ever created; this includes you the reader. The grace and mercy He has for all mankind is so amazing, and no one will ever treat you better than Our Father will treat us. No one can replace Him.

To each and every one of you reading this book: Just know that you have a story and a journey. Embrace your journey and just know that we are all brothers and sisters in Christ Jesus. Don't be afraid to share it, but embrace it and share it with boldness. The things that have happened to you happened for a reason, so take the opportunity to share your story. I declare that guilt, shame, fear, condemnation, brokenness or doubt will not hold you back from walking in your divine authority in Our Father. I declare boldness, strength, love, long-suffering, kindness, joy, hope, and a humble spirit to rule your life. Because of the blood I shed for you, you have been adopted into the Heavenly Family and we have a royal inheritance waiting for us. Know that our Father does not play favorites, but He loves us all.

To the children, obey your parents and your teachers. Learn as much as you can about our Holy Family and the role you play in the family. Please take the time to learn about me every day, to talk to me every day and to allow my precious Holy Spirit to lead and guide you in the truth.

We are all one big family and remember Our Father loves each of you!

www.ingramcontent.com/pod-product-compliance
Lightning Source LLC
Chambersburg PA
CBHW050444010526
44118CB00013B/1672